THIS IS
EGYPT

Contents

© All rights reserved
Distribution: ISIS for Import and Export, 52 El Zaher Street, Cairo Tel. (02) 910125
All rights reserved. No part of this publication may be reproduced in any form
or by any means without the prior permission of the copyright owner.
Photographers: L. Borodolin, W. Braun, B. Jackson, A. Colorni, I. Grinberg,
R. Eviatar, E. Maestro, Dr. D. Darom, Garo Nalbandian, J. Sahar,
K.F. Storheil, A. Giveol, O. Puukila, Image Bank p. 14, 108, 109
Pictures depicting objects in the museum are printed
by kind permission of the Egyptian Museum, Cairo.

ISBN 965-280-070-8

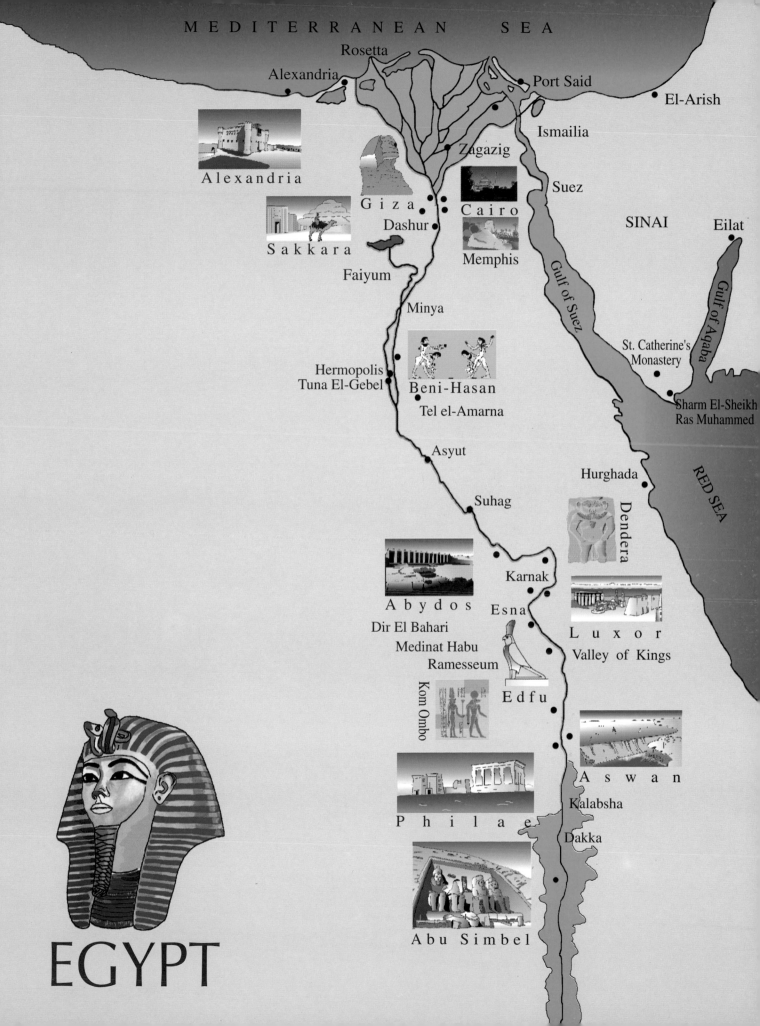

MEDITERRANEAN SEA

Rosetta
Alexandria
Port Said
El-Arish
Ismailia
Zagazig
Suez
SINAI
Eilat
Giza
Cairo
Dashur
Alexandria
Sakkara
Memphis
Faiyum
St. Catherine's
Monastery
Minya
Sharm El-Sheikh
Ras Muhammed
Hermopolis
Tuna El-Gebel
Beni-Hasan
Tel el-Amarna
Asyut
Hurghada
Suhag
Dendera
RED SEA
Abydos
Karnak
Dir El Bahari
Esna
Luxor
Medinat Habu
Valley of Kings
Ramesseum
Kom Ombo
Edfu
Philae
Aswan
Kalabsha
Dakka
Abu Simbel

EGYPT

INTRODUCTION

"There is no country that possesses so many wonders", wrote Herodotus, 2400 years ago. Egypt - the name brings to mind exotic images: pyramids and pharaohs, the River Nile and parched desert land, camels and sphinx, treasures of King Tutankhamen and the mysteries of a grand civilization that no longer exists.

Egypt lies in the north-east corner of Africa. From a bird's-eye view, the land appears as a lotus flower. The stem of the lotus is the Nile River valley - narrow and long, flowing from south to north. The glorious flower of the lotus is the Delta that spreads in the north. The rest of the country lies dry and barren, mostly arid desert partially covered by sand dunes. In fact, it is the eastern edge of the Sahara Desert. The Mediterranean Sea, which runs along Egypt's northern end, is linked to the Red Sea, a tributary of the Indian Ocean, by the Suez Canal, which borders the peninsula of Sinai.

Like the Sahara, Egypt would have remained desolate and parched without habitation were it not for the great Nile River which has determined the entire character and history of the land. The Nile is the longest river in the world. It flows along 6,700 kilometers from its source in the region of Lake Victoria to the Mediterranean Sea. The last 1200 kilometers cross Egypt. "The Nile winds in the middle of the desert with a fringe of green on each bank. This is the essence of Egypt," Flaubert wrote in a letter to his mother in 1850. In Cairo the river splits, creating a wide delta. In the past there were seven river branches but the great quantities of silt brought by the river led to blockage. Today only two exist.

Because Egypt is such a flat land, very few Egyptians ever see a mountain during their lifetime. This was certainly true during ancient times. It is not surprising, therefore, that the early Egyptians used a straight horizontal line as the hieroglyphic symbol for the word "land" when they referred to their country. Actually, the sign appeared twice with two parallel horizontal lines representing the "two lands", Upper Egypt and Lower Egypt - Upper Egypt is the Nile valley that runs along the entire length of the river, and Lower Egypt is the delta area, far to the north.

Although Egypt today covers an area greater than one million square kilometres, only 4 per cent of that is cultivated and inhabited. Almost the entire population lives on the banks of the river and the desert is empty except for nomadic Beduin.

opposite: The Sphinx
below: Sailing on a felucca on the River Nile.

The pyramids of Giza - Cheops, Chephren and Mycerinus.

GIZA - THE PYRAMIDS

"Four thousand years of history face you," said Napoleon to his soldiers as they stood at the foot of the pyramids. From the time of his conquest, at the dawn of the eighteenth century, Egypt was opened to the world - explored and excavated. Eventually it joined the community of nations as an important, independent country with great influence in the Middle East and Africa.

Seven wonders existed in the ancient world. All of them were man-made, but so colossal and memorable that they almost resembled creations of the Gods. Six were destroyed and vanished. Only one still stands in its place - the Great Pyramids of Egypt.

The pyramids were burial structures. They were not intended for mortals but for the Pharaoh himself, who was perceived as a God on earth. Upon his death, the Pharaoh was believed to leave the pyramid on his excursion to the Land of the Dead in the West, where he would unite with the Gods. His mummy remained in the pyramid with the fantastic riches that had been buried with him.

Every pyramid was built as a tomb for one, for Pha-

raoh alone. Thousands of labourers worked for many years to raise these gigantic mountains of stone. But the pyramids did not manage to safeguard either the deceased Pharaoh or his treasures. When discovered, they were found to be absolutely bare. Already in ancient times, robbers penetrated the pyramids, looted the contents and damaged the mummies.

Shapes of tombs changed with time. For most of the period before the first Pharaoh, known as Predynastic, it was customary to bury in a simple, shallow grave dug in the desert. These were covered with mounds of sand or a low pile of gravel to protect the body from animals and grave-robbers. It is possible to trace the continuous development both of ideas and architectural features from this simple grave to the great pyramids.

Towards the end of the fourth millenium BC, the pile of stones covering the grave was replaced by a construction of sun-baked bricks imitating the shape of a house. It contained rooms used for rituals and storage. According to their belief, it was the residence of the deceased. This structure resembled the wide bench built by villagers outside their homes - the "mastaba". Local inhabitants and scholars adopted the name for these burial forms.

There are three pyramids at Giza. The greatest belonged to the Pharaoh Cheops. Today it reaches a height of 137 metres but in the past it was nine metres higher. The peak of the pyramid is missing, as are the shiny casing blocks. On the top of the neighbouring pyramid of Chephren, the casing remains and enables us to reconstruct in our imagination the great beauty that the perfect finish contributed to this enormous edifice.

Until today the Great Pyramid is the largest structure that man ever built. It comprises 1,300,000 stones, the smallest weighing 2.5 ton each, and the largest about 15 ton each. The total weight of the pyramid is 6 million tons!

When Napoleon camped here with his troops, he amazed the soldiers with his calculation that the blocks from the three pyramids would suffice to build a wall 3 metres high and 30 cms. wide that could surround the entire country of France.

overleaf above left: Solar boat museum, Giza.
overleaf above right: A close view of a pyramid showing the enormous stone blocks.
overleaf below: The pyramids of Giza with Cairo in the background.
below: The Sphinx with the pyramid of Cheops in the background.

Ascending gracefully and elegantly along a sharp angle, with clean lines and unbelievable accuracy, the pyramid impresses not only with its size, but also with the feeling of stability and splendour it bestows on its beholders.

In the heart of the pyramid, at the end of a long gallery, is the burial chamber where the mummified body of the Pharaoh lay in a granite sarcophagus together with treasures of inestimable value. Today, only the empty sarcophagus is left in the room. One needs to muster all one's imagination in order to avoid disappointment upon reaching the choking chamber after a long and tiring climb along the narrow corridors and the gallery leading to it. Despite the great efforts expended to prevent looting - such as obstructing the passageways with huge blocks, camouflaging the entrance, and having the priests stand guard - nothing could stand against the tremendous temptation of the prodigious wealth.

Hundreds of years passed before the Pharaohs decided to hide their tombs. Until that time, towards the end of the Middle Kingdom, they continued to build Pyramids. Standing as silent witnesses to the mighty Pharaohs, there were almost one hundred all over Egypt. Most of them were destroyed.

The Valley Temple of Chephren, builder of the second pyramid, has been preserved in its entirety. Next to it is the famous Sphinx - symbol for foreigners of the mystery of Egypt. This divine creature, with the face of a king and the body of a lion, was carved out of a rocky prominence. This mystical statue, adorned with a royal head-dress, is believed by many to be a likeness of Chephren - it was meant to guard the pyramid and its temples. The sphinx was almost entirely buried by sand, until it was discovered and cleared at the beginning of the 19th century. Since then it has gazed at the world with calm oblivion.

below: *The temple and pyramid of Cheops*
opposite: *Cairo - the city of a thousand minarets.*

CAIRO

Cairo is one of the largest cities in the world and certainly the largest metropolis of the Mediterranean and all of Africa. Twelve million people live in Cairo but, during the day, an additional six million people come to work or do business in this bustling city. The overcrowding is astonishing and the noise overwhelms. Yet, this lively city is filled with charm and contrasts - a ride past modern hotels and skyscrapers brings you suddenly to the great pyramids; a stroll along the narrow alleys of the souks is followed by a ride to the suburbs on the brand-new metro. From the surrounding desert come the sandstorms that cover the city with fine dust and, since it almost never rains in Cairo, nothing ever washes it off the houses and trees, streets and parks.

Modern Cairo

The heart of the city is built along the Nile. At its centre is Liberation Square, Meydan el-Tahrir, bounded on the north by the famous Egyptian Museum of Antiquities, world famous for the treasures of Tutankhamen it houses within its 100 exhibition rooms. From the Square, Kasr el-Nil and Talaat Harb streets lead to the fashion and business sections, with the cinema centre behind. Across the square, the towering hotels block the view of the river. To the south stands Shepherds' Hotel, once the favorite of kings and queens, which was burnt as a symbol of colonialism in the 1952 revolution, but has been rennovated. Garden City, further south, was the former colonial residence. Carefully designed, with tree-lined streets, this neighbourhood is now the centre of embassies and residences which are built above the earliest pharaonic settlement in Cairo.

right: *Belly-dancer in a Cairo nightclub.*
below: *Cairo at night.*

Taking one of the many bridges across the Nile, one reaches the island of Gezira where the lotus-shaped tower of Cairo offers a good view of the entire city. The beautiful residential area of Zamalek has lovely parks and gardens. Here, in 1869, the Khediva Ismail built a palace to house Empress Eugenie of France and other royal guests at the opening of the Suez Canal. It has been restored and converted into a huge hotel.

The Cairenes love their city and many have never left it. This love is shared throughout the country and the city is the focal point of life in Egypt. Only on rare occasions do Egyptians refer to the city by its name. More commonly, they simply call it "Masr" - Egypt. For them, Cairo is Egypt.

Modern Cairo, teeming with people, alive with movement and the unbelievable noise of thousands of cars, trucks and buses is indeed the focal point and meeting place of three great continents: Europe, Asia and Africa.

The capital city of Egypt is almost as busy at night as it is during the day. Innumerable lights illuminate the streets. Chains of brilliant colours are reflected in the ever present Nile. The multitudes of people now no longer rush to work. The great swell of traffic has diminished, and the horns are silent.

Nightclubs are filled, and people stroll along the broad tree-lined avenues. The dynamic city offers something to everyone - history - sightseeing - sport - shopping - or just walking and imbibing the atmosphere of ancient and modern Cairo.

opposite above: The Mosque of Ibn Tulun.
opposite below: The Mosques of Sultan Hassan and Sibi el Rifai - amongst the finest examples of Mameluke art.
below: Partial view of modern Cairo with Tahrir Square in the foreground.

On top of the Mukattam hills stands the mediaeval Citadel which contains many structures, the most impressive of which is the Alabaster Mosque of Mohammed Ali built in the Ottoman style, flanked by two tall and slender minarets. Below lies the huge burial ground known as the City of the Dead which is filled with mosques, mausoleums and tombs of the Fatimids and Mamelukes. It is estimated that about one million people live in the graveyard, using the structures built around the family plots as homes.

The Alabaster Mosque was designed in the early 19th century by a Greek architect from Turkey - the style is based on the Ottoman mosques of Istanbul. The walls inside the building are decorated with alabaster brought from nearby quarries. Great chandeliers and glass lamps hang from low circular chains. They burn brilliantly, illuminating the richly coloured carpets and gilded decor of the great minbar or throne.

opposite: *Interior of the dome of the Mohammed Ali Mosque.*
right: *The tomb of Mohammed Ali.*
below: *The Mohammed Ali Mosque inside the Citadel complex.*

left: *Old Cairo - the round tower at the entrance to the Coptic Quarter. The Coptic Museum can be seen in the background.*

below: *The courtyard of the Islamic University complex of El-Azhar. This is one of the oldest, largest, and most important of the Islamic universities. There is also a Mosque in the complex, together with student dormitories, administrative offices and an inifirmary.*

The Egyptian Museum is probably one of the first stops for visitors to Cairo. Originally it was housed at Bulaq and then at Giza, until finally in 1902, it was moved to its present magnificent building. The museum contains a vast collection of pharaonic antiquities in its 100 exhibition rooms, notably the treasures of Tutankhamen. The displays are frequently changed, but various famous statues and objects remain in their set places. With the help of the museum catalogue it is not too difficult to identify them.

right: *The statue of the head of Hathor is situated in the Museum courtyard.*
below: *The Egyptian Museum.*

Group statue of King Mycerinus with a goddess of the 7th Nome (province) and the goddess Hathor.

Wooden statue of Sheik-el-Beled.

Ornately decorated throne of Tutankhamen showing the young King with his wife, bathed in the rays of the Amarna sun.

The Narmer Palette (1st Dynasty).
Menes, the first king of the 1st Dynasty is usually identified with the Biblical pharaoh, Narmer. He united Upper and Lower Egypt around 3100 BC and proclaimed Memphis as the capital. This slate stele was found in 1898. It is believed that it depicts the victory of king Narmer.

The gilded wooden shrine of the canopic jars for the internal organs of the mummified body.

Statue of King Amenophis IV. He later assumed the name Akhenaten.

Head of Nefertiti.

Seated statue of King Chephren.

To understand the story of Egypt more completely one must also visit the Museum of Islamic Art and the Coptic Museum.

Another place of interest is the huge Citadel Complex with its mosques and minarets. This was once one of the strongholds of the Islamic world. The construction was started by Salah-ed-Din in 1176 and finally completed in 1207. Today the great buildings and magnificent setting still inspire awe and admiration in all who visit them.

On the lighter side there are many pleasant walks along the Nile; a wonderful view to be enjoyed from the top of the Cairo Tower, browsing in the shops, a visit to the zoo, or just sipping coffee in one of the many coffee shops.

Khan el Khalili, the bazaar of Cairo, contains hundreds of narrow lanes jammed with stands and workshops offering shoppers a wide variety of goods as it has done for centuries. In the "Souk el Hiyam" section, tent-makers sit with crossed legs sewing colourful appliqued tents used for funerals or festivities. These can often be seen along the streets next to the mosques. Across the street from the market filled with bargaining tourists is the highly respected centre of Islamic studies, El-Azhar, with its twin-headed minaret.

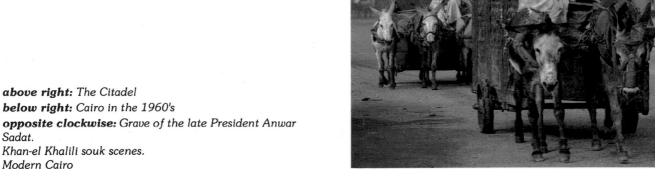

above right: *The Citadel*
below right: *Cairo in the 1960's*
opposite clockwise: *Grave of the late President Anwar Sadat.*
Khan-el Khalili souk scenes.
Modern Cairo

SAKKARA

Close to Memphis is the City of the Dead with the famous Step Pyramid, the oldest free-standing stone structure in the world. The Pyramid, which is six stories high, is surrounded by a wall. Inside, the tombs are decorated with stone friezes, fluted columns and painted reliefs. It was widely believed that this stepped pyramid represented a stairway to heaven.

opposite: Traditional agriculture
right: General view
below: The Step Pyramid at Sakkara.
inset: Pharaoh Djoser. The original statue is housed in the Egyptian Museum, Cairo.

The Pharaohs of the first two Dynasties were buried in large, fancy mastabas. The greatest pharaoh of the third Dynasty was Djoser (c. 2650 BC). With his ascension to the throne, he began building his tomb in Sakkara and preparing it for the day he would need it. Djoser appointed Imhotep - his Chief Vizier and architect, to direct the construction. He began by cutting an underground system of rooms out of the rock. Above them, he built a large mastaba using stone and not the usual brick. When this was done and the Pharaoh was certain that he had a tomb prepared, he gave instructions to enlarge and embellish the building. Imhotep extended the mastaba several times, but this was not enough. On top of it he built another five mastabas, one on top of the other, gradually decreasing in size. Thus a Pyramid of six steps that reached a height of 60 metres was created. This was the first pyramid and the first monument in the world built of stone.

Temples and an elaborate entrance building were built around it - all surrounded by an enclosure wall. In the stone-work it can be seen that the builders were not yet familiar with this material. They borrowed techniques from their work with brick, wood and reeds. But the beginning of construction with stone marked a radical change which soon allowed for buildings of enormous proportions - many of which have lasted until today.

People of that time, who had never seen a mountain, were excited and impressed by the pyramid - a man-made mountain. This achievement earned Imhotep the reputation for being a great genius and he was praised as a demigod for generations to come, also by the Greeks and Romans.

above: *Interior of the Pyramid of Unas showing details of the "Pyramid Texts".*
below: *Mastaba of Mereruka.*

above: Painted reliefs from mastabas in the Sakkara complex.
below: View towards the colonnaded entrance of the Step Pyramid complex of Sakkara.

The Alabaster Sphinx, Memphis.

MEMPHIS

Close to Sakkara is Memphis, the City of the Living, and the capital of Egypt until the end of the Old Kingdom, about 2,270 BC. It was built by Menes to ensure control of the newly conquered Delta, when he united Upper and Lower Egypt.

Today only a few broken columns and ruined buildings remain from this once flourishing town. The alabaster sphinx was discovered in 1912. It is thought to represent a king of the 18th Dynasty. Carved from a single piece of alabaster this huge statue was originally placed in front of the entrance to the temple of Ptah - where the ceremony of the crowning of the Pharaohs once took place. Housed in a small building nearby is a colossal limestone statue of Ramses II. The crown and the legs are missing now. Royal cartouches are carved on the chest and on the belt. Two delicately carved falcon heads decorate the handle of the dagger. Originally this statue stood in front of the temple entrance.

Another statue of Ramses II, 10 metres high, carved from Aswan granite, was found in the area.
In 1954 it was taken to Cairo and placed in the centre of the square in front of the station.
The King's cartouche is carved on one shoulder and on the belt of the statue. A smaller figure of his wife Bent-Anath is represented at the base of the colossus.

left and below: Statue of the great Pharaoh, Ramses II.
overleaf: Country life and methods of irrigation.

TUNA EL-GEBEL

The cemetery of Tuna el-Gebel provides examples of the burial tombs of the wealthy Greeks of Hermopolis. At about the time of the occupation of Egypt by Alexander (325 B.C.) the tomb chapel of Petosiris, the High Priest of Thoth was built. The outer facade is similar to that of a small temple and the burial chamber is in the centre of the chapel.

Finely painted wall reliefs depict traditional ancient Egyptian activities. These reliefs are much influenced by the contemporary art of the Grecian style. A tomb chapel resembling a modern house is close at hand. A large well for domestic water supply and the catacombs containing the mummified bodies of the sacred ibis and baboons are other important features of the necropolis of Tuna el-Gebel.

above: The tomb chapel of Petosiris, Tuna el-Gebel.
below: The columns of El-Ashmunein, close to the site of the Greek temple of Hermopolis Magna.

HERMOPOLIS MAGNA

The 15th nome of Upper Egypt was called Hermopolis Magna by the Greeks. Thoth, the god of writing, was the patron of the city. He is depicted as an ibis-headed man, an ibis or a baboon.

The temple of Thoth was situated in the centre of the ancient city and it had a portico with twelve columns.

Some of the red granite columns of the Greek Agora, one of the most important monuments, have been re-erected, but most of the city is now in ruins.

A TRIP ALONG THE NILE

The Nile River flows across the entire length of Egypt. In some parts it is so wide that residents along the banks call it "Bahr el-Nil" - The Nile Sea. It flows lazily, carrying on its back all types of vessels. Until modern times, the river was the main traffic artery - almost the only one. Since no settlements are found farther than a few kilometres from the river, it was much faster and easier to travel by boat. There was little reason, therefore, to use any other means of transportation - especially in a country as hot and rugged as Egypt.

It was so obvious to the early Egyptians that all their journeys and deliveries took place on the Nile that they didn't even have a word in their vocabulary for "travel". The expressions "to go up river", meaning to travel south, and "to go down river", meaning to travel north, were used even when referring to land travel. In hieroglyphics, the first was represented as a boat with a sail and the second as a boat with an oar. These signs were chosen because of the unique natural conditions of the river which greatly eased sailing on the Nile: the prevailing wind almost always blew from north to south while the river flowed from the south to north. So it was possible to use a sail when going upstream and to drift slowly or use oars to travel downstream.

Interior of one of the tombs. The roof is supported by four sixteen-sided columns. The statue niche can be seen in the far wall.

BENI-HASAN

The tombs hewn out of the rocks about 270 kms. from Cairo on the opposite bank of the Nile, take their name from the nearby village of Beni Hasan. There are thirty-nine tombs in all. They were quarried during the 11th and 12th Dynasties for local princes of the area.

The brightly coloured painted scenes of domestic life, sports, dancing and other leisure activities provide us with a detailed picture of the life of the Egyptians of the Middle Kingdom. Leaving the tombs and traversing a rough path, we come to a nearby rock-cut temple. This was built by Hatchepsut and Tuthmosis III for the lion-headed goddess Pekhet.

The temple follows the typical plan of a New Kingdom Sanctuary - religious scenes decorate the walls of the vestibule.

Sacred cats were buried in the cemetery close to the
temple.
Hermits and monks lived in caves, and were buried
in rock-cut tombs along the valley.

above: Entrance to caves.
below: The meeting of the Nile and the desert at Beni
Hasan.

TEL-EL-AMARNA

During the reign of King Amenophis in the first half of the fourteenth century B.C. a "revolution" occurred. The priests of the Amon temple in Karnak had achieved such a powerful position that they threatened the Pharaoh's authority. When Amenophis IV succeeded to the throne, he began a complex process that changed life patterns throughout Egypt. He declared that Amon and the other gods should be abandoned, and only one god, Aten the Sun god, should be worshipped. Thus the power of Amon's priests diminished. He created a new capital in El-Amarna, changed his name to Akhenaten and entirely altered the artistic style of the reliefs, floral motifs and representations of the cult of the Aten. Softer, freer lines were used in works of art that showed even personal domestic scenes such as the king with his daughter on his lap. The figures were no longer rendered idealistically and even the Pharaoh was pictured with a strange, elongated face. The changes lasted only during his lifetime. After his death, priests of Amon exploited the opportunity of having a young and ineffective heir, Tutankhamen, to renew the cult of Amon, to restablish the capital in Thebes and return life to its previous style. The new city of Akhet-Aten was soon forsaken, and quickly fell into ruin. Now known as Tel-el-Amarna, little remains of its ancient splendour.

left: *Statue of Akhenaten.*
below: *One of the caves at Tel-el-Amarna.*

ABYDOS

Since the commencement of the history of Egypt, Abydos has been a centre of pilgrimage and a place of important religious significance. Osiris, the judge and ruler of the netherworld, became the local deity at Abydos, and his cult was closely followed here. Every Egyptian desired, above all else, to make a pilgrimage to Abydos, and finally to be interred there in the precincts of the supreme god of the funerary cult. The splendid colonnaded facade of the temple of Seti I is dedicated to seven gods. Inside there are seven aisles for the funerary processions - a unique feature in temple architecture of Egypt. The columns and walls are richly decorated with larger than life-size reliefs.

above: Entrance to the Temple Seti I, Abydos.
left: Inside the Temple.

Wall painting with Seti I making offering to a deity.

Wall relief of the Nile god Hapy in the temple of Seti I at Abydos. The bunch of long-stemmed papyrus plants represents Lower Egypt.

DENDERA

A high brick wall surrounds the temple area at Dendera, isolating the complex from the secular world. Originally there were three sanctuaries, and three deities were worshipped here - Horus, Iky and Hathor. During the Ptolemaic period, new foundations were laid on the ancient site, and the temple of Hathor was constructed - one of the most notable accomplishments of late Pharaonic architecture, extremely well preserved to this day. These temples were built to the general plan of the earlier sanctuaries. The Hathoric columns are a special feature of Dendera.

Twenty-four massive columns are found in the great Hypostyle Hall. Each column is crowned by a portrait of the goddess Hathor. She has the face of a woman embellished with the ears of a cow.

During the Coptic period many of the capitals were damaged when the portraits of the goddess were defaced, but the splendour of the enormous hall has not been diminished. Hathor, the patroness of music and dancing, was worshipped in many forms. At Dendera she is usually portrayed in her most universal role - that of a slender young woman with the solar disc between two cows' horns worn on her head.

Standing in the inner courtyard of the Temple of Hathor at Dendera is the statue of Bes - an ugly, bearded and bandy-legged dwarf with shaggy hair and chin. He was a popular domestic deity, the patron of music and childbirth. The god of marriage and domestic happiness, he protected the people from evil. and was a great favourite in Egyptian homes - he was worshipped at local churches. Many charms, amulets and bracelets were made in his likeness.

General view of the Temple of Dendera.

The small hypostyle hall contains six huge columns with composite capitals surmounted by Hathor heads. The hall receives light from eight openings in the ceiling. Ceremonies that were performed at the founding of the temple are depicted on the walls.

Statues and the sacred barque of the deity were kept in the sanctuary. The wall decorations show the king undertaking his daily rites.

Every year the statue of Hathor was carried from the naos to the roof of the temple - these scenes are depicted along the walls of the staircases.

Reliefs of the Roman period adorn the outside walls of the temple. The beautiful Cleopatra and her son Caesarion are outstanding.

right: *The goddess Hathor*
below left: *Columns of the hypostyle hall surmounted by Hathor heads.*
below right: *The god Bes - protector of women in labour.*

HIEROGLYPHICS

The ancient Egyptians called their writing "Divine Words". They believed it was brought to them by Thoth, the ibis-headed god of learning and writing, scribe of all gods. A system of writing was essential to the Egyptian culture. Together with taxation, land division and other aspects of Egyptian life, the development of writing was inevitable. In fact, Egypt was one of the first places where this skill was practised, almost simultaneously with the appearance of writing in Mesopotamia. The form of writing in Egypt was very special - hieroglyphics.

At first Egyptian writing was pictorial. People drew what they saw, hoping others would understand the message or meaning. A network of schematic symbols, understood and accepted by all who used it, soon developed. Based on the earlier pictures, they retained their meaning. Most symbols stood for an entire word - an ideogram - that represented whatever was pictured: the sun, a bird, a hand, etc. Some of the symbols were used only to indicate the sound of the word - a phonogram. A combination of these sounds created a word. For clarification, a special sign (determinative) was sometimes added alongside the words to indicate that the symbol should be read as a unit, and not separately. The most familiar determinative is the oval frame - cartouche - around the Pharaoh's name.

In the early nineteenth century the young French scholar Jean Francois Champollion succeeded in deciphering hieroglyphics. He made use of the Rosetta Stone, found by soldiers of Napoleon's army 23 years earlier, which contained three identical inscriptions in three different scripts - hieroglyphics, demotic and Greek. Solving the mystery of hieroglyphics opened the doors to scholars who could now read the early texts found on the monuments and hundreds of papyrus that revealed in great detail much about the past.

opposite: *Feluccas sailing on the Nile. The Sanctuary of Hathor.*

View of Luxor Temple on the Nile.

LUXOR

Champollion, the scholar who deciphered hiero-glyphics, said of Luxor: "In Thebes the imagination of the Egyptians operated as though it was the imagination of giants. No people, ancient or new, has raised the art of architecture to such exalted stature."

Today, Luxor is a small town and only tourists fill it with life. But, after the throngs and commotion of Cairo, pastoral and pleasant Luxor is the most interesting place in Egypt. From every spot one sees fields and villages and the Nile is not caught among buildings and neighbourhoods but flows peacefully, its blue waters adding beauty and calm to this place. The temple was built and used over a period of many generations. Before reaching the shrine, one enters a large hall built by Amenophis III, at the beginning of the fourteenth century BC. The walls are decorated with reliefs showing the pharaoh with various deities. In the time of Alexander the Great, the columns of the hall were removed and a small chapel built within. Both outer and inner walls of the chapel were covered with reliefs showing the same scenes as on the walls of the hall. When one stands between the wall of the chapel and the wall of the hall - only a metre or two apart - it is difficult to notice any significant differences between the reliefs on them. Only a very carefully trained eye can pick out slight differences in the design of the foot, navel or others. And yet - the two walls were built and carved a thousand years apart! No other culture ever presented such stability and conservatism.

Little of the splendour and opulence, gates and walls, palaces, avenues and houses remain. Only the temple that once marked the centre of the city still stands on the shore of the Nile. Amenophis III began construction of the temple but parts of it, including the facade, were completed by Ramses the Great. Two of his seated colossal statues flank the doorway to the temple. Next to them stands one of the obelisks - a soaring monolithic granite column 23 metres high, weighing 227 ton. The matching obelisk was taken to the Place de la Concorde in Paris during the period of Mohammed Ali. In exchange, the French gave him a clock which was incorporated into the Citadel of Cairo. The Egyptians never fail to point out that it is not working!

The Avenue of the Sphinx, which was unearthed and excavated at several locations in various parts of the city, once linked this temple with the temple of Karnak, 4 kilometres farther north.

At the front of all Egyptian temples, monumental entrances were built - pylons. These were two high wedge-shaped slanted walls covering the entire width of the temple. Between them was the main gate to the temple. The walls were thick and usually had stairs within them, allowing one to climb to the top. The pylon was the most visible part of the temple and therefore it was completely decorated with scenes glorifying the pharaoh who built it. During the New Kingdom, important battles and victories of the Pharaohs were shown. In Ptolemaic times, the foreign Hellenistic kings portrayed themselves on the pylons receiving the blessings of the Gods. In so doing, they hoped to be seen in the eyes of their Egyptian subjects as legitimate rulers.

Comfortable local transport in Luxor.

Luxury hotel-liners take tourists on pleasure cruises, stopping en route at ancient sites. Smaller boats are used for local needs and ferries cross the river everywhere. Many of the boats use only sails. These flat boats, that can reach the shore at any place, incredibly resemble the ancient boats that appear on wall-paintings and reliefs. Today they are called "felucca" and are used for any purpose - transport and travel, fishing and even for tourists or travellers in search of adventure. Every felucca belongs to a private owner who works on it or rents his services to others. They adorn their boats, paint them and decorate the sails.

opposite above: Luxor Temple from the Nile.
opposite below: Ram's way leading to the Temple of Karnak.
below: Mosque of Abu'l-Haggag next to the court of Ramses II.

Archeologists and travellers in the last century found the monuments of ancient Egypt buried under drifts of sand. They were systematically excavated, carefully studied and reconstructed for generations of visitors. Many unique artifacts that would have been destroyed in other environments were saved, thanks to the dry climate: wooden utensils, woven straw, leather items and especially the papyrus which had been written and painted upon. The well-preserved papyrus, the wall paintings and reliefs of the monuments together with the abundant hieroglyphic inscriptions and records served as a rich source of information that enabled reconstruction of this truly great civilisation.

The precise rendering of detail in the paintings and reliefs enables identification of animal and bird species, furniture, and boat construction, observation of agricultural work and tools, etc. These prove that the Egyptian masters did not lack artistic technique but intentionally chose to base their style on strict adherence to a set of rules that would help satisfy a purpose higher to them than reality - to make things as complete as possible.

Proportions were calculated with exact measurements. The artist would divide the surface into a grid with a constant number of squares. The square was the size of the closed fist of the main figure. The head was equal to three squares, the neck - one, and so on for every part of the body. Proportions were clear and accepted throughout the generations.

opposite above: *Waiting for the ferry.*
opposite below: *The West Bank seen from Luxor.*
below: *Open court of the Temple of Luxor.*

KARNAK

The temple of Karnak is the largest religious complex in the entire world. It was continuously built by generation after generation, pharaoh after pharaoh, for 2,000 years. The principal deity worshipped in the Temple was Amon Ra, who became the most important of Egyptian Gods from the ascent of Thebes as the capital. Within this complex there are other temples, but the Amon is the largest and longest of all.

Ten pylons stand in the Karnak Temple, six of them along the main access of the temple, from west to east. Looking through the successive gates of pylons presents a breathtaking view through enormous halls and courtyards into the depths of the temple, where the sanctuary lies, 260 metres away. But, once you have crossed the temple threshold you face the confusion and complexity of buildings, pillars, statues, obelisks and hundreds of metres of inscriptions and reliefs accumulated over two millenia.

The most celebrated and spectacular feature of Karnak is the great hypostyle hall that covers 6000 square metres - large enough to hold within it both St. Peter's Church of Rome and St. Pauls' Cathedral of London or the entire Notre Dame of Paris. A forest of 134 columns supports the ceiling. All are decorated with religious scenes, as are the walls and ceiling. The two central rows of columns are raised higher than the others to allow air and light to enter through windows on either side. These columns stand 23 metres high - equal to an eight storey building - and are wide enough to have at least six people stand around them with their outstretched arms touching.

This hall was built by Sethos I and Ramses II - pharaoh of the exodus story in the Old Testament. Despite its powerful dimensions, the hall is not at all oppressive. In fact, the feeling is one of celebration and respect. True, people are dwarfed by the immensity, but they feel comfortable. There is no doubt that the planners and builders meant to give believers a sense of awe before the Gods, but also intended the hall to convey the sense of harmony which was essential to the Egyptian view of the cosmos, where each and every man had his place.

opposite: Entrance to the Temple of Karnak, after the 1st pylon.
below: Karnak from the Sacred Lake.

The outer walls of the hall, which could be seen by the masses, are covered with scenes of various kings, their military campaigns, victories and captured prisoners. These reliefs and the Pharaoh's chronicles elsewhere in the temple present an incomparable historical source. Much of our knowledge of Egypt and its neighbouring countries come from them. They also recall stories of the Bible.

Across the hall, past more pylons, stands the tallest obelisk in the world - a thirty-nine metre high monolithic needle of red granite. Its twin, that once stood nearby, did not survive and fragments lie scattered about. These obelisks were built by a queen who was one of the most colourful figures in Egyptian history - Hatchepsut - who ruled around 1500 BC.

❧

When an Egyptian made a statue of a god or goddess, pharaoh or nobleman, his purpose was to have this likeness embody the subject at his best for eternity. Therefore, no transient features such as feelings, expressions and movement were shown. The essence and meaning were more important than the form and fleeting moment. Art was rational and not emotional, idealistic and not realistic, intended to transmit a message, not to represent appearance. No attempt was made to be faithful to reality in their portrayal. Rather, they deliberately changed it in order to clarify and emphasize the symbolic image - the idea that was to be perpetuated.

The Pharaoh was always presented as taller than all other humans to stress that he was the most important of all. The human figure was not presented from a single viewpoint using perspective, but rather as a composite with each component shown from the angle which best displayed its shape and nature. The face is most easily viewed in profile. The eye is most clearly seen from the front. So, in both paintings and carved reliefs the Egyptian artists placed a full-view eye within a side-view face. Feet and legs were always shown from the side.

It was understood that the Pharaoh could not be in all places at once. The priests who served in the temples were his representatives. But his likeness was always found in the form of a statue to act as mediator between God and man. With time, the priests gained strength and accumulated great wealth. So did the commanders of the army. But never did their power reach the level of the Pharaoh's and without exception, he alone was seen as the absolute ruler.

opposite above: Sound & Light Performance.
opposite below: The Ram's Way, Karnak
overleaf: Hypostyle pillars at Karnak.
below: Temple of Tuthmosis, the Festival Hall.

VILLAGE LIFE

About half the population of Egypt lives in villages along the shores of the Nile and in the Delta area. Small towns serve as regional centres for the villages. Together they form a long strip of settlement stretching almost uninterrupted along the entire length of Egypt. The small villages, called Naaga, merge today into larger units, the balad. But villagers still live in small, simple houses built of mud-brick, branches and cane. On low hills, the village houses are crowded together - each with its own courtyard in which the chickens and children run around. Cows and water buffalo return from grazing and enter the yard for the night. After milking, the women of the house prepare butter, cheese and sour milk in a sa'an - a goat-skin churner hung on a tripod of sticks in a corner of the yard. Daily, they bake a special pita-bread, esh, in an oven made of mud and bricks - the tabun. The service buildings such as the cow-shed, storage areas and kitchen are built around the courtyard. The bedrooms are always on the second floor - open to cooling breezes and removed a little from the flies and mosquitoes. When the sons marry, they come back with their brides to join the extended family in the paternal home.

Electricity, and sometimes running water, is supplied to the houses by the government. More often, young girls come to draw water from wells that supply cleaner water than the river. They carry it back

opposite clockwise: The colossus of the High Priest of Amun, Pinudjem I, originally a statue of Ramses II, with a female statue portrayed between his legs.
Statue in front of pylon.
The fallen obelisk of Hatchepsut.
below: *Columns of closed papyrus buds.*

home on their heads in well-balanced jugs. Most villages are built at some distance from the river, beside one of the main irrigation canals. The women of the village gather on the bank of the canal to wash their clothes and the men come to pump water for their fields. They hoist up their galabiyas - the traditional dress worn by men-and direct the water to small canals dug in their fields and flood one plot after the other. Across the country the cultivated areas are sectioned into flat beds appearing like a giant chess board. The land is tilled with simple ploughs pulled by oxen, and only recently have tractors appeared in the fields.

opposite left: *The Rams' Way.*
opposite below: *Statues of Ramses.*
below: *Wall engraved with many cartouches of pharaohs of Egypt.*
right: *Remains at Karnak with obelisk in the background.*
Overleaf: *Views of Karnak*

Scenes from village life.

COLOSSI OF MEMNON

Because the cult of the king had to continue after his death, the temple had to be accessible to both priests and believers. Since the royal tombs were in a hidden location, the temples were built away from the tombs, on the western edge of the green valley, bordering the area covered by the annual innundations. They appeared large and impressive when seen from the capital city on the opposite bank. Colossal statues of the king were placed in front of these mortuary temples. The most famous are "The Colossi of Memnon" named by the Greeks for the legendary hero of the Trojan War. Actually, they are statues of Amenophis III whose temple once stood here, but vanished.

Hewn from single sandstone blocks, the statues, over 20 metres high, gaze out over the Nile. The Pharaoh is represented seated on his throne in the classical position, with his hands resting on his knees. Their fame spread throughout the Greek and Roman world - especially because one of them emit-ted a great sound when warmed by the morning sun - like a giant sigh. This sound was probably made when hot air escaped through the cracks in the stone. After repairs were carried out under the order of the Roman Emperor Septimus Severus, the phenomenon disappeared. Today both of the statues are badly weathered and in a poor state of repair.

left: The Colossi of Memnon.
below: Villages amidst the caves and tombs of the West Bank.

DEIR-EL BAHRI

Hatchepsut was married to her half-brother, Tuthmosis II. After his death, she ruled as regent together with her step-son, Tuthmosis III. Actually the young pharaoh was powerless and she governed alone as a true pharaoh. Since it was required of the pharaoh that he be a man, Hatchepsut appeared as one and was so portrayed on all of her statues and reliefs. She built herself a mortuary temple on the west bank of the Nile which differed in plan and shape from all others. The temple, known today as Deir el Bahri, was planned for her by the influential architect, Senenmut. It is built into the mountain cliffs as three wide terraces, adorned with statues and pillars, rising up towards the sanctuary that is cut out of the rocky hillside.

The temple in the shadow of the Theban hills is one of the loveliest in Egypt. Its reliefs depict not even one military episode but rather show unique scenes such as a trade expedition of boats returning from Punt (Somali) loaded with exotic potted plants, African animals and plenty of gold for the pharaoh. Also depicted is the transport of her gigantic obelisks from the Aswan quarries to Karnak - four hundred kilometres north. The obelisks, weighing 320 ton each, were brought by special boats tied together to create a large raft. During innundation, the rafts were brought as close as possible to the quarry

opposite clockwise: Relief on walls depicting journey to Punt.
Fallen masonry in temple courtyard.
Pillars of Hathor.
below: Deir-el-Bahri, the Temple of Hatchepsut.

and later to the temple. But, it was still necessary to incorporate great strength, with the help of ropes and many people, to get these gigantic rocks onto the boat, into place in the temple and at last, the hardest task - to stand them upright, After the queen died, Thutmose III wanted to blot out everything relating to her reign. He destroyed many of the wall reliefs at Deir-el-Bahri, and replaced her figure and name with his own. Much of the complex was disfigured and destroyed, but the temple dedicated to Hathor suffered the least damage. Recently, Christian monks lived in the monument, caring for it and preventing further destruction.

left: *Hatchepsut suckling from goddess Hathor.*
below: *Relief of the goddess Hathor.*
opposite clockwise:
Relief showing Hathor rattle.
Offering table with God Amun.
Tuthmosis III, stepson of Hatchepsut, offering libation to Horus.
overleaf: *Temple of Hatchepsut.*

MEDINAT HABU

The Mortuary Temple of Ramses III, one of the world's largest monuments, is second only in importance and size to Karnak. A stone quarry used to occupy the site on the West Bank of the Nile. During the Christian era a village sprang up - later excavations uncovered the remains of a city built around the Pharaoh's palace. The present day complex consists of four temples: one built by Amenhotep I, one built by Queen Amenartas, and two built by Ramses III in the 20th Dynasty. The enclosure was reached through the High Gate - built along the lines of a migdal or fortress gateway in the style of Syrian architecture. Wall reliefs depict the king doing battle with his enemies.

We also see the great Pharaoh in Paradise - wearing the unadorned clothes of a simple farm worker he ploughs his land, performing without fatigue, one of the necessary duties of the deceased, in order that he may be granted eternal life by the gods.

The temple of Ramses III is believed to be built on the site of Djamy, the sacred home of the eight primordial gods. It is a jewel of perfection, a classic example in lay-out of an Egyptian temple of the period. It contains two pylons, two courts, a hypostyle hall, two smaller halls with columns, and a sanctuary with additional rooms in the vicinity.

The entrance pylon to the temple of Medinat Habu.

The peasant's lot in life was usually poor and without many privileges. But bitterness and anger were not widespread. They believed and accepted that all citizens - and even the land itself - was the private property of the Pharaoh. He alone could talk to the Gods and direct the rituals. In fact, on all reliefs and wall paintings the Pharaoh is seen alone in front of the Gods. The blessings of the Gods - life, eternity, stabilty, wealth - were bestowed not only upon him but also upon his subjects and his land. So, it was in the best interests of all to continue the rituals and see that the gods would take care of their Pharaoh so that they, too, could reap the benefits.

Painted roof with hieroglyphs of the kings.
opposite above: *Medinat Habu.*
opposite below: *Sakhmet, the goddess of war. Statue in the temple of Medinat Habu.*
below: *wall painting - Ramses III wears the white crown of Lower Egypt, and the red crown of Upper Egypt.*

THE RAMESSEUM

The warrior king, Ramses II, has perpetuated his name through the length and breadth of Egypt by the vast temples, pillars and statues which bear inscriptions and reliefs of his achievements. During the 67 years of his reign in the 19th Dynasty, Ramses II dedicated his enormous funerary temple to the god Amun. Many of the mudbrick storehouses and offices have crumbled into decay and although the buildings that remain are badly damaged, it is still possible to follow the layout of the temple complex. The walls are adorned with reliefs showing battles against the Hittites at Kadesh, and with pictures concerned with Min, the god of renewed life and fertility. Massive pieces of masonry lie scattered in the courtyards, a reminder that the monument had once been used as a quarry.

right: *Fallen head of Ramses II wearing the double crown and Osiris pillars of the hypostyle hall of the Ramesseum. Entrance to the tombs of the Valley of the Kings.*
below: *The Mortuary Temple of the Ramesseum - Deir-el-Bahri.*

VALLEY OF THE KINGS

Hatchepsut had a tomb hewn for herself under her temple on the west bank. But it is unclear if she was buried there or in a tomb she had prepared in the Valley of the Kings beside the graves of her ancestors. During the New Kingdom, all pharaohs' tombs were set in a hidden valley behind the cliffs on the west bank of the Nile in Thebes. The robbery and vandalism that the early tombs had suffered deterred the pharaohs from continuing the same burial system. The pyramids signalled to all: "within lies the sarcophagus surrounded by incredible treasures".

In order to avoid damage to the tomb, the mummy or the treasures, they decided to hide them in a secret, unknown place. Long, slanting tunnels led to the burial chamber carved deep within the rock. After the coffin and riches were placed in the chamber, the corridors were filled with gravel and earth in an attempt to hide the tombs from the eyes of pillagers. Openings were camouflaged and many tricks used to mislead potential looters - false chambers, sudden changes of direction along the path, and so

on. A special village was built for the workers and artisans employed in construction of the royal tombs. This village, today known as Deir el Medina, was isolated from the world so its residents could not pass on the secrets of the valley.

However, all these efforts were in vain. Nearly all the tombs were robbed. Luckily, the priests collected and hid some of the mummies which have survived until now, among them the mummies of Hatchepsut, Tuthmosis III, the famous mummy of Ramses II and other great pharaohs.

The long corridors leading to the burial chambers of the pharaohs were covered with carvings, murals and texts showing the king's journey to the afterlife where he would unite with the Gods. Most show the pharaoh and other Gods on the night voyage of the sun and demons who threaten her from every direction. None of these incredibly beautiful scenes were intended for the eyes of mere mortals. All was done only to aid the deceased.

Through the efforts and determination of one archeologist, Sir Howard Carter, one almost entirely untouched tomb was found. It was the only one ever discovered that had not been looted. This tomb, belonging to the Pharaoh Tutankhamen, was found in

Entrance to the tombs of the Valley of the Kings.

1922 after eighteen years of tiring and frustrating searches. Without a doubt, this was the most exciting and richest discovery ever made in Egypt.
Twenty-five hundred articles were found in the tomb. Many were made of gold and others of ivory, silver, alabaster, wood, etc. Hundreds of precious stones were inlaid and the total value is inestimable. The inner coffin alone was made of 110 kilograms of pure 24 karat gold. But, even more astounding than the value is the beauty of the artifacts - all works of art with great charm and splendour. Today they occupy a special place in the Egyptian Museum of Cairo. Hundreds of thousands stood in line at museums around the world to see the King Tutankhamen collection when a special exhibition of the finds went on tour.

opposite: The death mask of Tutenkhamen.
above: The golden coffin of Tutenkamen.
below: Interior of the tomb.

This entire collection belonged to one young and rather insignificant king who died - probably assassinated - in his youth at 18. His tomb was very small when compared to the graves of any other pharaoh - only the walls of the burial chamber were painted. The pictures are not as well preserved as those of other tombs. On the wall opposite the sarcophagus are paintings of the King presenting himself to the gods of the Netherworld. The other wall shows six of the twelve baboons who represent the twelve hours of day, and the twelve hours of night.

above: Horemheb with the god Anubis.
below: The Pharaoh paying homage to a deity.

Over long periods of time Egypt was isolated and had limited contact with the world outside. Surrounded by deserts that separated it from neighbouring countries, yet inherently rich and blessed, Egyptians developed a unique and independent civilisation. They saw themselves as the gods' favourites. People living in the fertile countries beyond the desert were "the wretched who depend on rain and yearly seasons".

Death was not seen as the last step. They believed that beyond life in this world there was continued physical existence, not only of the soul but of the body as well. But, this destiny was not automatically assured. They believed that the Pharaohs - as divine rulers - would join the gods in the afterlife. However, even they would have to surmount dangers along the way and face the judgement of the gods. This is shown on many tombs and papyri as a scene where Thoth, the god of wisdom and divine scribe, holds a scale on which he balances the heart of the deceased against Ma'at, the goddess of truth and justice. The judgement took place in front of Osiris, Lord of the afterworld.

The tomb of Ramses VI.

The Sarcophagus Chamber.

According to Egyptian mythology, Osiris was the first Pharaoh on earth and ruled together with his beloved sister and wife, Isis. They brought much to the world civilisation, including agriculture, law, art and piety. Their popularity and success aroused the jealousy of their brother, Seth, who murdered Osiris and usurped the throne. Seth then cut the body of his brother into fourteen pieces and scattered them around the world in order to prevent Osiris from coming back to life. Isis, the faithful wife, set out to gather all the parts of her husband's body. After succeeding in doing so, she used her magic power to resurrect him. Osiris did not want to return to this world and preferred to become King of the Afterworld. Isis bore him a son, Horus, the falcon-headed god, who was the rightful heir. But he had to fight Seth and revenge his father before regaining the throne.

above: Representation of the sky goddess Nut painted on the ceiling, protected by Nadjet, the goddess of Lower Egypt.
overleaf: Decorative frieze with winged solar disc.
A white clad attendant holds a sheet of metal to catch the sun's rays, and reflect them into the innermost depths of the tomb - a simple and effective way of "making light".

THE VALLEY OF THE QUEENS

Under the burning sun, amidst the stark beauty of the stones and boulders we find the Valley of the Queens - connected to Deir-el-Medina by a short stone track of about 1km.

Here the Queens, princes and princesses were buried in tombs similar in construction to those found in the Valley of the Kings. The tombs are decorated only with paintings - no reliefs have been found.

The walls were covered with mud from the Nile, the surface was made smooth and then whitewashed. The riot of brilliant colours seem to have been painted yesterday, instead of some thousands of years ago.

The tomb of Prince Amen-Hor Khepesh-ef, the young son of Ramses III, is outstandingly beautiful. The Sarcophagus chamber is lavishly decorated with paintings of the young prince and his father.

below: The Tomb of Amen-Hor-Khepesh-ef (the son of Ramses III). The Pharaoh is introducing his young son to Dwamutef, the jackal-headed son of Horus. The young prince wears the traditional sidelock of a youth, and carries a ceremonial plumed fan in his hand.

VALLEY OF THE NOBLES

The tombs of the nobles, much smaller than those of the kings, were carved in rock and decorated with completely different drawings than the royal tombs. No scenes of the journey to the Afterworld are depicted. Since the nobles could not afford to ensure that they would be buried with plentiful possessions or that after death people would continue to bring them essentials such as food and clothing, they guaranteed their future by representing all things they would hope to have in life after death. These provide us with detailed pictures of daily life during the New Kingdom - agricultural scenes, hunting and fishing, palatial festivals, musicians and dancers, maids and servants, craftsmen and artisans, etc.

Tomb of Ramose. Relief of Ramose and his wife Satamon.
Ramose was an important vizier at the time of the revolution of Akhenaten. His tomb in the Valley of the Nobles is adorned with beautiful reliefs on many different subjects. Perhaps the loveliest shows Ramose and his wife paying homage to Osiris, and later to Akhenaten and Nefertiti. The style is classic - the same themes can be seen at Amarna.
opposite: *Well-preserved paintings on the walls of the tomb of Sennefer in the Valley of the Nobles. He was the overseer of the gardens of Amon during the reign of Amenophis*

THE VALLEY OF THE ARTISANS

The Valley of the Necropolis workers is set apart from the other tomb areas. The houses are surrounded by a wall. The artisans lived in the sprawling village: stoneworkers, engravers, quarrymen and artists all worked here.

right: *The tomb of Inherkha. Four identical, sophisticated Anubis gods painted on the arched roof of the burial chamber.*
below: *Remains of the village of the necropolis workers.*

Inscriptions and figures on remnants of pottery found in the area tell us something about life in the village.

The houses were long and narrow, nearly always with an upper floor. Sometimes a storeroom and terrace were added.

The workers built their own personal tombs, always beautifully decorated with paintings on the walls and often on the ceilings.

above: The tomb of Sennedjem.
Painted scenes of Sennedjem and his wife working in the fields of Paradise (Iahu)..

below: Osiris, the god of death, with the eyes of Horus
The green-faced god of the Netherworld, judge and ruler of the dead, wears the atef-crown, and holds his symbols of office - the flail and the crook.

left and below: The tomb of Sennedjem. Husband and wife, both with perfume cones on their heads, worship the gods of the after-life.
opposite clockwise: *The foot ironer.*
The snake charmer.
Transporting sugar cane by rail.

ESNA

On the west bank of the Nile thirty miles south of Luxor is the small town of Esna. The Ptolemaic temple standing on the site of the 18th Dynasty temple is built well below the level of the present day town. The complex was dedicated to the ram god Khnum, who shaped the human body and was also the god of the Nile flood. The only part of this temple which is still standing is the vestibule with its ornately decorated capitals. The names of the two Roman emperors, Vespasian and Claudius, are recorded in the hypostyle hall which was built during their rule. There are twenty-four great pillars more than ten metres high. Each pillar is almost entirely covered with hieroglyhics texts, and is capped with a composite capital of a floral design. The temple is somewhat dark and gloomy.

The mixed columns of the vestibule and hypostyle hall at Esna. The capitals are ornately decorated with elaborate sculptures of various plants and flowers.

EDFU

Continuing along the west bank of the Nile, about seventy miles south of Luxor, is the small town of Edfu. Here we find one of the best preserved temples in Egypt.

The great cult temple of Edfu was rebuilt during the reign of Ptolemy III. The foundations were laid in 237 BC and building continued over two centuries, and was finally completed in 57 BC. The temple of Edfu was dedicated to the sun god Horus - the golden falcon; the goddess Hathor, and their son.

The basic plan of the temple complex remained unaltered over the centuries. Additions were not made as in the temples of Luxor and Karnak. The cult temple of Horus portrays Egypt in miniature. The threshold of the country is represented by the en-

above: The sacred barque, Edfu.
below: The great pylon at the entrance to the Temple of Edfu.

trance pylons. These are nearly always adorned with great reliefs of the pharaoh playing or capturing his enemy. Inside the temple there is usually a huge forest of gigantic pillars in the hypostyle hall. The ceilings are decorated to represent the firmament. Symbolic manifestations of gods and local plants are everywhere.

right: Black granite (holy of holies) naos inside the sanctuary at Edfu.
below: The courtyard at Edfu - Horus wears the double crown of Upper Egypt and Lower Egypt.

The west bank of the Nile is no longer perceived as the land of the dead. Cultivated fields, as in the past, still stretch across every inch of irrigated land. Sugar cane is now the main crop of Upper Egypt, harvested by hand, then loaded on camels who bring it to railroad trucks. It is then hauled to local refineries. But today, unlike in the past, many villages are built on this side of the river. Houses are tucked among the noble tombs, beside and above them. The government has attempted to move the villagers from the area rich in antiquities, but the residents refuse to leave this enduring source of wealth. Tourists come in droves and are invited to visit the many craft shops and restaurants, to buy souvenirs and - for a little "bakshish" (tip) - visit the tomb in a private home which, of course, was long ago emptied of all its contents.

Agriculture formed the basis and foundation of life and economy in Egypt. Such a dry area depends on irrigation for cultivation. From the beginning of the floods until the end of autumn sufficient water was absorbed by the fields.

Great quantities of mud and silt, rich in both minerals and organic material, were carried by the strong streams. Every year the receding waters left behind a new layer of rich soil. This dark earth gave the name to the living land, blessed with the gift of the Nile - "The Black Land" - as opposed to "The Red Land" - desert covered by sand and stone, gleaming red in the hot sun. The Egyptian farmer never needed to worry about fertilization or crop rotation. Anything planted or sown in this rich alluvium flourished in the natural conditions of rich earth and abundant water combined with a warm, predictable climate.

One of thousands of irrigation channels leading from the Nile.

The temple of Kom Ombo.

KOM OMBO

South of Luxor, standing on high ground over-looking the Nile is the temple of Kom Ombo. From most parts of the temple complex one can glimpse the Nile with feluccas passing by. The plan of Kom Ombo is traditional with entrance pylons, vestibules, hypostyle hall and sanctuary, but unlike any other temple in Egypt, it is shared by two deities. Sobek the crocodile god and Haroeris - Horus the great, the god of war, are both worshipped here. The Ptolemies rebuilt Kom Ombo in the second century BC on the site of a temple that was erected during the reign of Thutmose III.

The temple complex is encircled by an outer wall which has two doorways leading to the Nile. There is a lovely view from the terrace. An imaginary boundary line divides the temple in two parts, giving each god his own abode. Haroeris is worshipped in the left part, and Sobek in the right.

Little remains of the entrance pylons and the walls of the court. The vestibule, however, has a highly decorated facade with ornate columns of carved stone. Reliefs of the sacred crocodiles can be seen in the hypostyle hall. Perhaps the most bizarre feature of the complex of Kom Ombo is the mammisi. This is not in a good state of repair now, but we can still see the undamaged mummified crocodiles that were placed there so many centuries ago. A nilometer - an ancient gauge to measure the innundation of the Nile is still visible on the side of the bore that leads directly to the river.

left: Remains of the columns in the courtyard of the temple.
below: The nilometer

ASWAN

A boat travelling south along the Nile can sail easily and uninterrupted for 1200 kilometres until it reaches Aswan. South of Aswan, the river is not navigable. It is not the High Dam of Aswan that blocks the way. Below the dam, still within the boundaries of the city, the Nile cuts its way through the hard granite rocks which are exposed in this area and splits into many winding rapids. This is the first cataract - one of seven found between Aswan and Khartoum in the Sudan. Today the cataract is mostly buried below both the High Dam and the lake created by the old dam, while the second cataract is completely submerged in Lake Nasser. In ancient Egypt, since the river was the main transportation route, this natural barrier formed the southern border. Actually, today it is still the end of the road since, even though the recognized border lies further south, Aswan is still the southernmost city.

Another small island, to the west of Elephantine, was once the headquarters of Lord Kitchener, conqueror of Sudan. It is now a lush, botanical garden full of exotic trees and flowers, thriving under the tropical skies of Aswan. On the western bank, the dunes of the Sahara reach down to the river. High above is the Mausoleum of the Agha Khan, the hereditary leader of the Ismaili sect of Islam centred in Pakistan.

overleaf clockwise: The Botanical Garden on Kitchener's Island.
White sailed felucca passing the Aga Khan Mausoleum.
General view of Elephantine island.
below: *General view of Aswan, with the Cataract Hotel in the foreground.*

Until the High Dam at Aswan was built in 1970, every summer the seasonal flood waters of the Nile would innundate Egypt. The summer monsoon rains in the Ethiopian Highlands brought vast quantities of water - about 60 billion cubic metres - flowing along the eastern tributary, the Blue Nile, to the main river. In the past, the raised water would completely cover the entire river valley and delta. The inhabitants built their homes in high places to avoid destruction. The fields disappeared under the water and only after three or four months reappeared. In anticipation of the oncoming floods, the farmers would build high dykes around the fields to stop the water and dig canals to distribute it as much as possible. The water lasted a long time and was absorbed into the ground. It could be used by the farmers for their crops long after the floods had ended.

Their dependence on the annual innundation and need to predict accurately the time of its occurrence, necessitated careful observation of the cyclic pattern which led to increased astronomical knowledge and early development of a yearly calendar. The Egyptians were the first to divide the year into 365 days - 12 months of 30 days each with 5 extra days at the end for celebrations. Within these unique conditions, other sciences such as arithmetic, mathematics and

Views of Aswan.

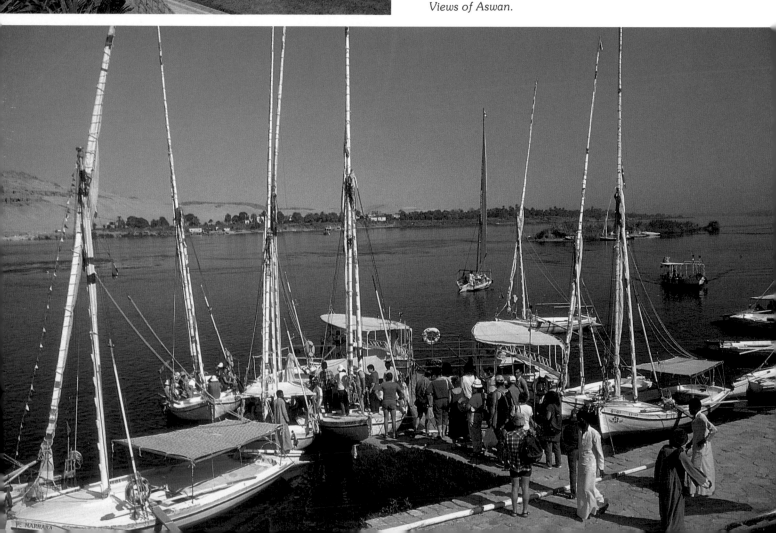

geometry also reached a high degree of sophistication to answer the need to measure angles and gradients, plot paths for canals and redivide washed-out fields. This great civilisation, shaped by the river, achieved incredible feats that enabled it to build the pyramids.

From the very beginning, Egypt's economy was based on agriculture using the waters of the Nile. Administration of the waters and control over them were always important tasks for the ruler and a source of power. But, enormous quantities of water were lost when they flowed and disappeared into the Mediterranean during the annual floods and only a small portion was therefore available in the country that had very little rain or other source of water. To take advantage of some of that water, the British began building a dam in Aswan, at the end of the last century. Today it is referred to as the Low Dam or the "old one". By catching some of the floodwaters behind the dam and creating a reservoir, it

right: *The lotus flower monument in Aswan. Carved from grey granite, the memorial represents lotus flowers united by a workers wheel. It was erected to commemorate the united efforts that finally achieved the building of the Aswan High Dam.*
below: *The generating station at the High Dam.*

was possible during the dry season to use water that would normally have flowed down the river to the sea.

The dam increased the areas of cultivation and allowed for an ambitious system of irrigation which led to higher yields. But the population of Egypt increased at a higher rate. When the British dam was being built, the population of Egypt was 11 million. Today, it has reached over 50 million! Every year there are an additional million Egyptians; every day three thousand new infants are born. Only one generation ago Egypt exported a lot of its agricultural products and rated high among world food producers.

The residents of Aswan are predominantly Nubian. Tall and black-skinned, they incredibly resemble the pictures of their forefathers, carved in the temple walls. The Nubians have lived in this area and further south throughout Egyptian history, and many of their traditions remain unchanged. Ethnic crafts such as knitting, beadwork and basket-weaving are still popular. Nubians have their own spoken language which is not used for writing and reading. It is used alongside the more common language of Egypt, Arabic. But, there is no doubt that the Nubians are an integral part of the Egyptian nation.

The crowded city of Aswan has faced serious changes since the construction of the High Dam, but the old magic can still be found wandering through the "souk" (open market) where the fragrant spices fill the air and the well-laden stalls tempt both locals and tourists.

The granite found here had great importance from the earliest periods. The Pharaohs, builders of the pyramids, took great pains to bring huge blocks of red granite from Aswan to Giza, a distance of 1000 kilometres. The burial chamber of Cheops in the heart of the Great Pyramid is built entirely of exactly matched large granite slabs. Chephren, Cheop's successor, built his valley temple beside the sphinx and faced it with large granite stones brought from Aswan. The granite quarries were used throughout history and the largest obelisks were cut here. In one of the quarries an unfinished obelisk can be found. Had it been finished it would have been the largest of all - 42 metres high, weighing no less than 1150 ton! It was intended, it seems, to decorate one of the buildings of Hatchepsut - the incredible queen who ruled hundreds of years before the Iron Age, around 1500 BC. Workers used hard, stone hammers of diorite in their endless work of slowly, continuously pounding the rock until it was pulverized to dust. Then, after all that hard work, a crack was found in the obelisk and the workers were forced to leave it in place, where it sits today, nearly 3500 years later.

above: The Nubian market.

left: The unfinished obelisk. Queen Hatchepsut odered this obelisk to be erected, but it was never completed. Cracks started to show in the great block of granite - and it was decided to leave it "in situ" in the north quarry.

PHILAE

Amelia Edwards the British Egyptologist wrote about Philae: "with its palms, its colonnades, its pylons, Philae seems to rise out of the river like a mirage." This description no longer applies. Philae, the last refuge of the cult of Isis, the religion of the Pharaohs, has been dismantled and resited on the island of Egelika, safe from the inundation of the waters of Lake Nasser. Construction of the temple dates back to the 30th Dynasty. The Ptolemies and the Romans completed the building. Philae was dedicated to the goddess Isis - the sister and consort of Osiris, and her son, Harpocrates - "Horus the child". After Christianity was recognized as the religion of the Roman Empire, the cult of Isis was still secretly followed for many years.

In a similar procession to that of Horus at Edfu, the statue of Isis was taken in a sacred barque from her

left· The first entrance pylon to the temple of Philae.
below: The Island of Egelika with the temple of Philae.

temple at Philae to Rigga, an island where her husband Osiris was believed to be buried. Parts of the Ptolemaic temple are well preserved, while other parts can hardly be distinguished from the surrounding rocks.

When the Christians converted this temple into a church during the 6th century, shocked at the voluptuous form of the goddess, they covered these reliefs with mortar. Religious texts were written over them and crosses were inscribed. During restoration of the temple the mortar was removed and the reliefs appeared, fresh and undamaged.

The kiosk of Trajan is probably the most well known part of the temple of Philae. This much enlarged facsimile of a shrine for the sacred barque is normally found inside the temple sanctuary. Fourteen magnificent stone columns with intricate floral-headed capitals stand ready to receive a covering roof. When processions came to the island to celebrate religious festivals they passed through the kiosk on their way to the temple. Today the processions are groups of tourists who come to marvel at the perfection of the temple of Philae.

opposite and overleaf below: The Kiosk of Trajan, Philae.
opposite overleaf: Lake Nasser.
below: The open courtyard of the temple of Philae.

ABU SIMBEL

Today the waters of the Nile leave the dam via the six concrete tunnels of one of the largest electrical power stations in the world, which supplies most of the Egyptians' energy needs. Lake Nasser covers an area that once held many Nubian villages. Inhabitants were transferred to new towns built especially for them north of Aswan.

With the construction of the High Dam nations of the world united under the auspices of UNESCO to help Egypt save many ancient sights that would otherwise have been submerged. The most famous effort was the race to save the fabulous temples of Abu-Simbel from the rising waters. Unlike most other temples, Abu-Simbel was not built, but was hewn out of the rocky cliffs.

The entire cliff, including the temples carved within and the four colossal seated statues of its grand facade, were sawn into huge blocks that were transported and rebuilt on higher ground situated not far from the original site. Today the temples appear almost as they did in the past - as an integral part of the cliff - and it is almost impossible to detect the cuts in the rock. Past the impressively gigantic stat-

ues are the darkened temple halls, supported by columns which are floor-to-ceiling statues of Ramses in the posture of the god Osiris. The walls are beautifully carved and painted. In the sanctuary there are 4 images of deities including one of the Pharaoh himself. Twice a year the first morning rays of sunlight enter the sanctuary and light the gods just as they did at the original location.

opposite above: *Facade of the Temple of Hathor, Abu Simbel.*

opposite below: *The Osiris Pillars of Ramses II. Osiris pillars representing Ramses II support the ceiling of the main hall. Hewn from the natural rock, two long rows of four columns each stand on either side of the central passageway. The King's arms are crossed and he wears the double crown of Egypt on his head*

below: *To the left and right of the entrance to the temple, Queen Nefertari is flanked on either side by statues of her husband, the great Pharaoh Ramses II. At their feet stand smaller statues of their children.*

Outside the temples a small door is located at the side of the cliff. After entering, you pass along a corridor until suddenly, you are inside an enormous concrete dome. Then - and only then - is it possible to really comprehend the magnitude of this undertaking. The dome is the heart of the mountain, built by the engineers who feared loading the entire weight of the rock on the temple after it was cut and rebuilt. One cannot miss being impressed by the extent of this marvelous engineering feat. The feeling of excitement is further enhanced outside the dome when, taking another look at the temples, you face two breathtaking achievements - accomplished with a time span of over 3300 years between them.

The tomb served as the eternal home of the dead where he would continue to require all that had been available to him on earth - including basics such as food and clothing as well as luxury items such as perfume and games. It did not include living people - slaves and servants. Human sacrifices were not customary in Egypt nor the killing of servants so they could join their master upon his death. Instead, statuettes of servants - ushebty - placed in the tomb were expected to perform all tasks. During burial, all these things were put into the chamber with the mummy. Later, offerings were brought to the deceased by relatives and priests.

opposite clockwise: The sun god Re-Horakhty above the entrance door to the Great Temple.
Nefertari, represented as a small figure protected by her royal spouse.
Relief figures of the god Hapy, the Nile god of fertility. Below them, note the group of prisoners roped together.
Statues of Ramses II by the entrance door.
below: The Temple of Abu Simbel at night.

KALABSHA

With the construction of the Aswan High Dam, other monuments of Nubia were threatened with oblivion - to be submerged by the rising waters of the artificially made Lake Nasser.

A salvage team established through the good offices of UNESCO, financed by West Germany set to work in 1961. The temple of Kalabsha was the first to be dismantled.

Hugh sandstone blocks were numbered and taken by barge to their new site 14 kms south of Aswan. Here they were re-erected on a granite promontory, safe from the threatening waters.

The temple was dedicated to Mandulis, a Nubian form of the god Horus, and the cult of Isis was also practiced here.

above: *The court of the Temple of Kalabsha.*
left: *Capital of a Hathor column from the Kiosk of Qertassi nearby.*

ALEXANDRIA

In the year 333 BC Alexander the Great conquered all of Asia Minor, penetrated Syria and reached the gates of Gaza - the only city in the area to resist. After Gaza was captured, the last barrier blocking Alexander from entering Egypt was gone. The Persian governor of Egypt, completely cut off from his homeland, surrendered to Alexander. The Egyptian priests, who had suffered from a lack of tolerance under their previous rulers, the Persians, received Alexander with open arms. He offered sacrifices to the Egyptian gods and went on an expedition to the desert oasis, Siva, to consult with the Oracle of Amon. In Memphis, the capital, Alexander was ordained as the Pharaoh, King of Upper and Lower Egypt and Lord of Two Lands.

Thus Alexander became another link in the long chain of Egyptian rulers and took upon himself the traditions and customs of Egypt. Alexander did not attempt to dictate a new way of life and extend Hellenism here as he did in other nations he con-

above: *The Corniche - Alexandria - the "Pearl of the Mediterranean".*
left: *Montaza Palace.*

quered. Instead, he adapted himself to the accepted norms and framework of life which had remained almost unchanged until then. He built and renewed temples for the local gods, had his name and titles inscribed in hieroglyphics and his likeness carved on reliefs as a pharaoh in every sense and in the style of Egyptian art with no hint of the developed Hellenistic art of his homeland and people.

Egypt was the richest land Alexander conquered and his income from it far exceeded that from any other place. In order to connect Egypt with the centre of his empire, he decided to establish a new port city on the Mediterranean Sea, built in his name - Alexandria. The location for this new city was chosen at the western edge of the delta, in a place protected naturally from the great mass of silt that flows with the Nile to the sea.

Modern Alexandria is still a lively city, the second largest in Egypt, with ships from foreign ports arriving regularly and over a million people flocking annually to spend their summers at this resort. But, there is little left of the once glorious Greco-Roman city which was the cultural capital of the entire Mediterranean. A small theatre, Pompey's Pillar and the catacombs are the only witnesses to the lost grandeur.

right: *Pompey's Pillar - This was once part of the sanctuary of the temple of Serapis. A single rock of rose-pink granite from Aswan has been fashioned into a magnificent pillar, topped by a Corinthian capital.*
Near the pillar is a sphinx - one of a pair - carved from pink granite.

below left: *Fort Qait Bey. The 15th century fortress was built with stones from the lighthouse of Pharos, situated where the lighthouse once stood before it was destroyed by a tidal wave after an earthquake.*

below right: *Roman theatre discovered in 1964.*

HURGHADA

This is becoming a main tourist centre on the Red Sea. Clear blue waters, guaranteed sunshine and a beautiful beach add up to the perfect holiday resort.

First class hotels provide all modern amenities. Fishing, diving, snorkeling and other aqua activities are all available for the energetic holiday maker.

LIFE IN THE RED SEA

There are over one thousand species of tropical fish in the Red Sea. Multi-coloured corals and brightly-hued fish delight the eyes of the scuba divers in this underwater paradise. Coral reefs fringe the shore-line, the water is crystal clear and the sun shines eternally.

Boat building in Hurghada
below & opposite: *Water sports and beach scenes*
overleaf: *Underwater views of the Red Sea*

THE SUEZ CANAL

The ancient Egyptians recognized the significance of a canal between the Red Sea and the Mediterranean. Making use of the Nile delta, Ramses II tried to establish this connection. Many schemes were started and abandoned. From the writings of Herodotus we learn that some 120,000 Egyptians died whilst working on these projects.

In 525 BC the Persians invaded Egypt. King Darius I completed the work on the canal, which, however, soon fell into a state of disrepair.

Trajan restored the canal at the end of the 18th century renaming it Trajan's Canal. Once more it was neglected, silted up and fell into disuse.

The project was taken up by the Suez Canal Company, who started work in April 1859, finishing ten years later after overcoming many problems. The Suez Canal was officially opened with much pomp and ceremony on the 18th November 1869.

Quite considerable charges are levied for the use of the canal. Nevertheless it is one of the world's most used waterways.

RAS MUHAMMED

Ras Muhammed at the apex of Sinai - about 18km south of "Sharm-el-Sheikh" lies between the two gulfs of the Red Sea - the gulf of Aqaba and the gulf of Suez.

High coastal mountains surround the rocky bay, which is sheltered from northerly and southerly winds. The flat, table-line shelf suddenly ends with a sheer drop to the coral reef some 30-50 meters below. This is considered to be one of the best diving centers in the world today.

The whole area has been made into a vast nature reserve, with strict attention paid to the preservation of the natural wonders that abound. Camping is only permitted at the designated sites; swimming and diving are only at recognized spots.

The shark observatory is a popular must for visitors. Standing on the rocks one looks down to see the many sharks swimming lazily in the clear water below.

A natural canal penetrates inland for 500 meters - on either side of it are the most beautiful mangroves in all of Sinai.

right: Views of Ras Muhammed.
below: The Suez Canal.

Sharm-el-Sheikh.

SINAI

Many events of Biblical history are believed to have taken place in the varied and beautiful landscape of the sparsely populated Sinai Peninsula.

In ancient times the Pharaohs searched here for gold and precious metals. On one of its mountains, Moses received the Ten Commandments. Christians persecuted under the Roman Empire found sanctuary in the rugged mountains.

SHARM-EL-SHEIKH

The Sinai Peninsula is a vast area of untamed beauty. Great strides have been made to modernize this hitherto neglected territory. Seaside resorts have been established where visitors can relax and enjoy the sunshine or the beautiful sandy beaches. For those who are more energetic there are aqua sports, diving and snorkeling. Hotels, cafes, nightclubs and restaurants cater to a cosmopolitan crowd of holiday makers searching for "sun and fun" - away from the hustle and bustle of town life.

DAHAB

The traveller of today searches for natural beauty, tranquility and sunshine - Dahab has a full measure of all three. One of the most magnificent coral reefs in this area is to be found near the date palms of the Beduin village of Dahab.

The Coral Island
left: Dahab.
below: Diving in the Red Sea.

ST. CATHERINE'S MONASTERY

St. Catherine surrounded by high mountains believed by some to be the Biblical Mount Sinai, and today is home to a group of monks belonging to the Greek Orthodox Church. The peace and tranquility of this monastery instill a feeling of deep piety in the hearts of those who live and work there. Many treasures are kept in the library and the museum. The Church houses a wonderful Byzantine mosaic of the 6th century.

Perhaps the most well known part of the Monastery is the Chapel of the Burning Bush.

TABAH

The border crossing between Egypt and Israel was established at Tabah in 1982. A luxurious, modern hotel close-by provides all the comforts and amenities necessary for a "sunshine holiday". But the landmark of Tabah must surely be the well-known multi-trunked Sudanese Palm. Silhouetted against the sky-line the palm stands sentinel over the sand dunes. This is the most northerly point where the species is found.

BEDUIN

The nomadic Beduin of the desert are mainly wandering herdsmen. They live in their tents almost as their ancestors did in Biblical times, surviving the rigours of heat and lack of water.

Tents are woven from the hairs of the black goat - this is the work of the women. During the summer many families build shelters from desert shrubs.

The camel is still a prized possession, being used for transport, providing camel-hair for clothing, and cheese and milk for food. Beduin life is simple, the entire wealth of the family is invested in their flock of goats.

Times however are changing - Beduin families now often live in permanent housing, many own cars and vans instead of a camel. Children study in permanent schools, some even carrying on to university.

Whatever happens, hospitality is still of prime importance to the Beduin. Passers-by are warmly welcomed, and invited into the tent or home. They are given small cups of strong, bitter coffee, followed by glasses of steaming hot, sweet tea. The Beduin will give his last piece of bread and share his bowl of food with his guest - a sign of truth and true friendship.

above: Tabah Hilton Hotel.
opposite above: St. Catherine's Monastery
opposite below: Mt. Sinai.
overleaf: Scenes from Bedouin life.

127